THE FORGIVENESS BOOK

THE
FORGIVENESS BOOK

healing the hurts we don't deserve

D. PATRICK MILLER

Foreword by FREDERIC LUSKIN

Cover design by Jim Warner
Cover photograph © Jing Jing Tsog/the ispot
Interior photos/images by Vecteezy and FreePik
Interior by Steve Amarillo/Urban Design LLC
Typeset in Monotype Centaur and Sackers Gothic

Hampton Roads Publishing Company, Inc.
Charlottesville, VA 22906
Distributed by Red Wheel/Weiser, LLC
www.redwheelweiser.com

Sign up for our newsletter and special offers by going to *www.redwheelweiser.com/newsletter/*.

ISBN: 978-1-57174-777-8
Library of Congress Cataloging-in-Publication Data available upon request

Printed in the United States of America
M&G
10 9 8 7 6 5 4 3 2 1

TABLE
OF CONTENTS

FOREWORD

When first published as *A Little Book of Forgiveness* in 1994, this was a book whose ideas and message were ahead of its time. At that time there were only one or two published scientific studies demonstrating the power of forgiveness to make a difference in the lives of people who forgave. In 1994 my own thinking about forgiveness was mostly latent; I was unsure of just how important forgiveness was to the well-being of body and mind. I would not attempt my first research project until the end of 1996, and even then my thinking was rudimentary and lacking in power.

I have directed the Stanford Forgiveness Projects for the past eighteen years. These are a series of research endeavors that helped substantiate the power of forgiveness to reduce hurt, depression, anger, and stress in people who hold grudges. In addition, the Forgiveness Projects have shown that forgiveness can reduce the physical manifestations of stress, reduce blood pressure in angry hypertensives, improve physical vitality, and improve one's compassion and optimism. The Projects have also shown that forgiveness is for everyone; we conducted research on hurt college students, angry and disappointed middle-aged adults, stressed-out business people, and people who have had family members murdered by political violence. In addition to this research, I have taught forgiveness to tens of thousands of hurt and angry people.

What I find fascinating is that the things I taught, researched, and proved to be true, D. Patrick Miller already knew. I am writing this foreword because of the remarkable degree of concordance this book has with the results of my research. The huge number of people I have worked with clinically demonstrates to me that the simple truths espoused in Mr. Miller's work are just that: simple truths.

One example of many is Mr. Miller's understanding of the power of gratitude. He writes this straightforward suggestion to establish the importance of this relationship: "To accelerate forgiveness, practice gratefulness." Then he goes on to describe the power of gratitude in his own life and how that has improved his ability to forgive. In our forgiveness methodology and my self-help book *Forgive for Good: A Proven Prescription for Health and Happiness,* gratitude is a central concept. My experience has shown that the ability to feel gratitude is directly related to people's ability to forgive; grateful people seem to have an easier time letting go of their harsh judgments.

What I like about this book is that I can pick it up at any page and get an insight that is helpful in understanding and moving towards forgiveness. It does not matter where I begin or for what I am looking; each page resonates with some truth about the subject and is written in a gentle and inviting manner. It is clear that this book has emerged from personal experience and a depth of practice. Reading *The Forgiveness Book* will offer the reader a safe and guided passage into a practice that is essential for mental and physical well-being. As Mr. Miller highlights so movingly, the more of us who practice forgiveness, the more people who are available to heal both our world and ourselves.

Frederic Luskin, PhD
Author, *Forgive for Good* and *Forgive for Love*
Director, Stanford Forgiveness Projects

INTRODUCTION

Is there anything going on in your life that just wears you out? A thankless job, a chronic illness, a troubled relationship? Have you gone over and over this situation or circumstance without finding a solution or a way out?

When a problem resists solving, it's often because we have unknowingly limited the range of possible solutions. That happens because we have looked at the problem in the same way for a long time. Forgiveness begins with the willingness to look at any difficult circumstance of your life in a new way. Forgiveness is not about letting anyone off the hook for a mistake, insult, or crime. Nor is it about trying to forget something that bothers you. In fact, forgiveness may first require that you look more deeply at whatever is bothering you, because looking more deeply at something in particular will be the first step into seeing everything differently. And seeing everything differently is the way of forgiveness.

When this volume was first published as *A Little Book of Forgiveness* in 1994, there was indeed something "little" in the way that I approached my subject matter. While learning and practicing forgiveness had made a profound difference in my life, I was still a little worried about pushing the idea too hard—as if it might be impolite to suggest too strongly that other people could benefit from giving up a grudge or changing a vengeful outlook. Less than a decade into my own spiritual discipline at the time, I was somewhat tentative about promoting all the advantages of it.

Fifteen years later, I decided to revise and re-title the book in light of the greater understanding of forgiveness that I had developed since. This is the sixth edition over twenty-three years, during which I've realized that far from being a little undertaking, forgiveness is a disciplined and increasingly joyful approach to seeing and being that amounts to a new way of life. Nowadays I have a much better idea of what that means than I used to. The way of forgiving certainly doesn't mean becoming weak or passive, or using forgiveness to avoid conflicts. It does mean increasing one's capacity to deal with challenging relationships and daunting circumstances, because less energy is wasted on pointless resentments and rehashing ancient injuries. Gradually, a habitually cynical state of mind can give way to a happier and more spontaneous response to the world.

Still, adopting forgiveness as a way of life does not mean becoming a saint who sees only the best in everyone. In fact, it may actually sharpen your perceptions of people's flaws and failings, including your own. But when you see these problems with compassion rather than judgment, your own strength is immeasurably increased. Over time, what once seemed like shortcomings in another, or yourself, may be seen merely as differences that need have little or no negative impact on you.

This is the "magic" of forgiveness: the gradual lifting of sad and weighty judgments that may have once seemed absolutely necessary, without actually having served any useful purpose at all. As you learn to let go of unproductive judgments, your stress level will decrease, freeing up more positive energy for creativity, relationships, and the general enjoyment of life. Forgiveness is not the end of all stress and struggle, but it is an effective antidote to alienation and despair.

The first part of this book presents a specific prescription for how to go about any particular act of forgiving. The Seven Steps of Forgiving given are not the only way, but they provide a practical method that has proved reliable in my experience. In three somewhat arbitrary divisions, the rest of the book indicates how it may feel to adopt forgiving as a way of life. Feel free to read pages at random; ideas that are linked are marked with Roman numerals: I, II, III.

At the end of this volume, I've expanded on the Seven Steps with more specific instructions that can be used on your own or in group study. I hope readers can use the ideas in this book the way I use them: as seeds for inspiration that lead to both personal and social change. I'm sharing what

I've learned about forgiveness so far and forecasting where it may lead, but the particular messages I'm passing on are less important than the messages that readers receive while trying out this book. In a sense, I'm attempting to help others become attuned to the frequency of forgiveness: a clear tone of sane inner guidance in a world filled with the harsh static of fear, confusion, and vengeance.

At different times in my life, I've tried to change the way that others thought and behaved, through reporting, creative expression, and argument. But only forgiveness has substantially changed *me* for the better—by making me less angry and self-absorbed, and thus better able to relate to people fairly and compassionately. I hope that the changes that have come through me also come through clearly in this book. If even a few readers are inspired to release some old and unforgiven pain in their lives, I will be a satisfied and ever more inspired activist.

—D. Patrick Miller

SEVEN STEPS
OF FORGIVING

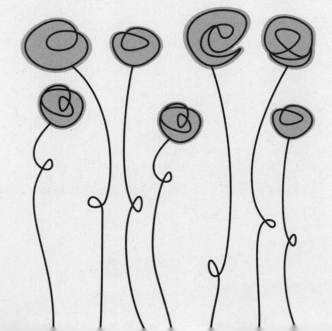

Select a bitter sorrow, a serious grievance against someone, or a punishing charge against yourself, and review it in complete detail.

Hold in your mind the image of whatever is to be forgiven—yourself, another person, a past event—and say, "I release you from the grip of my sadness, disapproval, or condemnation." Concentrate quietly on this intention.

Imagine for a while what your life will be like without the sorrow or grievance that has been haunting you.

4

Make amends with someone you've hurt or someone who has hurt you; tell a friend about your self-forgiveness; or otherwise bring your inner work to your relationships.

5

Ask for God's help to overcome fear or resistance at any step. If you do not believe in God, ask for help from nature, humanity, and the mysteries of your own mind. These are the channels through which aid is sent—and aid is always sent.

Have patience. Forgiveness induces healing which follows its own order and timing. Whether you think you have accomplished anything thus far is less important than the fact that you have attempted a radical act that will call forth change likely to exceed your expectations. Go about your daily business, but stay alert to unexpected shifts in your thinking, feelings, and relationships.

Repeat steps 1 through 6 as often as necessary, for life.

(See the end of this book for additional suggestions on following the Seven Steps.)

FORGIVING
OTHERS

It might seem a lot
easier to forgive
someone if only he or she
would show signs of changing.

The paradox is that we are unlikely to see signs of change in
others until we have forgiven them. This is true for two
reasons. First, resentment is blinding. It limits our perception
of what is real now—and what may be changing right in
front of us—and shuts down our capacity to envision a
happier future. Second, a subtle but crucial function of

forgiveness is that it tacitly gives others "permission" to change. We are not nearly so separate from each other as we generally experience ourselves to be. We think that we grow and change only within ourselves, but we also grow and change partly within others, and they within us. Some people may find very little space within themselves to change, and need others to let them into a psychic territory of forgiveness, where they can feel free to try a new way of living.

Soon after I had begun forgiving my parents for all the wrongs I thought they had done to me—without saying anything to them about it—they seemed to become more open and frank about their personal history, everything that had influenced them to become who they were. At certain moments the extent of their revelations was stunning, and I wasn't sure of exactly what was happening. Had I heard these things before without paying attention, because of my

We all change together

resentments at the time? Or did my parents feel permitted to tell me more about themselves because I was showing them signs of greater acceptance than I ever had before?

Now I believe that both kinds of change were occurring, and this evolution continued. I'm no longer concerned about which change was theirs, and which was mine. We all change together if we change at all. This overlapping of each other is easiest to experience in a couple, family, or other close relationship, but I think it's true of the family of humanity as well.

That's what makes forgiveness so powerful. Anyone can initiate the changes we all need by opening up new territories within his or her mind—our one mind, really—where others can find the room to take a deep breath, start telling the truth, and shake off the cloak of guilt they have so long mistaken for their own skin.

if we change at all.

Begin not with the idea that you are doing a favor to someone who hurt you, but that you are being merciful to yourself. To carry anger against anyone is to poison your own heart, administering more toxin every time you replay in your mind the injury done to you. If you decline to repeat someone's offense inwardly, your outward anger will dissipate. Then it becomes much easier to tell the one who hurt you how things must change between you.

"Forgive and forget" is a popular distortion of the work of surrendering grievances. The real process is "Remember fully and forgive." If it were actually possible to forget everything you forgave, you could teach very little to others seeking freedom from their resentments.

It's true that we eventually forget some things we've truly forgiven. But that kind of forgetting takes care of itself; it's not something you can tell yourself or anyone else to do. Trying to forget is just a form of denial—and whatever is denied is not forgiven. Remembering fully helps us take note of what we do not want to see repeated, so that forgiveness doesn't inadvertently give anyone permission to commit the same mistakes again.

Begin not with the
idea that you are
doing a favor to
someone who hurt
you, but that you
are being merciful
to yourself.

When you are trying to decide whether someone deserves your forgiveness, you are asking the wrong question. Ask instead whether you deserve to become someone who consistently forgives.

Examine carefully the temptation to catalog, classify, and frequently update the file of "Wrongs Done to Me." The only case you will build is one against yourself, as you increasingly believe in secret that you deserve what you're getting, even as you complain about injustice.

Living in forgiveness means yielding your grip on misery. Many people feel that it is this grip that makes them authentic and serious; such is the melodrama of the adolescent soul. The mature soul empathizes with misery only to connect with those in suffering, and lead them to forgiveness. When I was young I spent a lot of time with friends commiserating about the state of the world, the problems with people we knew, and everything else that added up to the general difficulty of being human. Forgiveness taught me to notice when I was drifting into pessimistic bull sessions, and to seek a more useful direction for conversation. I don't want to be insufferably optimistic, doing a hard sell of happiness while losing my connection with anyone who may still subscribe to suffering. I have to keep one foot planted there, at the ground level of another's discontent. But with the other foot I try to step up or out in a new direction. I guess I might be a better exemplar of hope if I were more confident of where I'm going. But it might also be that people are moved more by another's tentative willingness to see things differently than they would be by a dramatic declaration of a better way. Perhaps watching someone learn to change makes a more lasting impression than having someone try to save you.

Forgiveness may be stern or soft, reassuring or discomforting, eloquent or clumsy. The first expression may be incomplete and need restatement or elaboration to be understood by others, and made clear and strong in one's own heart. Perfection is not a prerequisite for attempting to forgive.

"Sweet revenge" is junk food for the soul. The brief rush that revenge provides will always be followed by the degradation of one's character. There is a real joy to be found in setting things right, but that always involves changing oneself for the better first.

To find your missing creativity, release a little of your attachment to the worst injury ever done to you. Grieve the deadness that you are letting go of, and that you have so long regarded as a trophy wound. Then celebrate the opening of a door through which your childlike nature can come back to you, laughing, asking the simplest questions, clearing your vision.

In a time when the recollection and classifying of abuses has become a virtual industry, we have to be careful about proclaiming the specialness of our wounds. The end point of remembering exactly how we have been damaged is to realize that we all share the deep common wound of humanity: being born into vulnerable bodies in a mysterious and dangerous world. Our particular wounds have a lot to do with who we are, and that history is important to understand. But learning to forgive all our wounds, regardless of their severity, is what will speed us toward our potential. An

Forgiveness is

the first breeze

of early spring,

carrying an

unexpected warmth.

unimagined creativity blossoms in every space within the heart from which pain has been released.

Forgiveness is the first breeze of early spring, carrying an unexpected warmth.

Don't be alarmed when resentment returns after you think you have thoroughly released someone from blame. Our attachment to fear runs deep, and the thought of holding no grudges whatsoever loosens fear's grip. Then it whispers in our ear that forgiveness might steal away our old familiar world of isolation and suspicion. Whenever you find a good reason to reinforce an old grievance, ask yourself what fear has actually done for you lately.

In the forgiving relationship, the struggle over power is replaced by the mutual impetus to serve. Jealousy dissolves into playfulness, suspicion into helpfulness, and possession into shared freedom.

Forgiveness will not save every relationship, but it will allow an inner healing to proceed even when a rift is inevitable. We are always relating to the whole of humanity, and to Creation itself, through the specific channels of our relationships. To forgive is to remember that we cannot separate ourselves from the whole.

Relationships that seem to fail represent the reeducation of your expectations. Forgiving others for hurting or disappointing you begins with understanding how you have chosen your teachers.

The most efficient expression of forgiveness answers attack as it happens, neither by condoning nor by opposing it, but by staunchly offering correction of its senselessness.

The martial art of aikido teaches that an attacker is always off balance, and that the goal of defending oneself is really to return the attacker to a peaceful state—laid out on the floor, if necessary. If we can learn to see all attackers as aspects of our selfsame humanity that are not yet in balance with the whole, then we can instinctively respond to attacks with acts of compassion that are as firm as they need to be, without violating others or ourselves.

I

A robber steals because he thinks something has been stolen from him. If we hope to rehabilitate him rather than reinforce his violent habit, the message of our rehabilitation efforts must be:

Things are not as they seem; you have everything you need within you.

Anyone trapped in illusion is healed by seeing through it, not by being schooled in a harsher illusion. All criminals need a better metaphysics, a wiser foundation for their thinking.

How to forgive a murderer? First, by differentiating his sufferings from his exploitation of death to ease them. For his sufferings—greed, jealousy, frustration—he will need reeducation, support, and compassion. For our outrage about murder, we need to examine deeply our faith in death. As long as we collectively believe that death has power over life, we will spawn deluded, self-appointed little gods who want that power.

Time heals some wounds, but major wounds can permanently change our sense of self. It may seem that we have little influence on what a crime or catastrophe does to us, but we do have the choice of responding with bitterness or wisdom. That choice is seldom clear at first, because the first step toward wisdom may include accepting our bitterness for a while.

Time heals
some wounds,
but major wounds
can permanently
change our
sense of self.

You are perfectly entitled to remain angry and
resentful for as long as you like. You are perfectly entitled to
believe you've been cheated or denied, that everything is
ruined, and that you will always be under the thumb of

misery until other people miraculously change (which they won't do, of course). Best of all, you are perfectly entitled to get so tired of believing all this that you decide to change miraculously on your own.

If you want to be merciless, be merciless against the temptation to blame. Question the usefulness of blaming at every opportunity. Ask yourself, "If I had committed a crime, would I respond better to condemnation or caring?" If you find within yourself a secret desire to be condemned, ask yourself what needs to die within you. Chronic self-blame is always a means of putting off the work of change.

I

Make no mistake: anyone or anything that seems to have control over you is experienced as a momentary stand-in for God. Every grievance, regardless of degree, is an argument with divine creation, the fundamental power that made things the way they are. In other words:

> When you are mad at anyone, you are mad at God.

When you are mad at God, it is crucially important to admit it. This saves many potential victims from your anger, redirecting it toward Someone who can transform it and heal you.

II

It is difficult to stay mad at God, because most of the time our experience of God is nothing more than an idea. Yet our consciousness itself is nothing more than an endless rush of ideas about reality. In this view, forgiving God means exchanging many useless ideas for one idea that works.

The grudge against God—or in nonreligious terms, the grudge against reality—is the keystone grudge for all of one's unhappiness. I've learned that I can save a lot of time by following the connections of all my petty, middling, and major grudges back to the keystone grudge, and then asking myself the question, "Is it more likely that God was wrong to make the world this way, or that I am somehow wrong in the way I'm looking at it?" If I decide that God was wrong—or that there is no God and I am merely the victim of an uncaring, mechanical universe—then there isn't much

I can do. But when I realize that I can always clarify my perceptions of the world, I can start learning and contributing again. That seems to be the way to both humility and power.

FORGIVING
YOURSELF

I have experienced
two fundamental
ways of being in
the world.

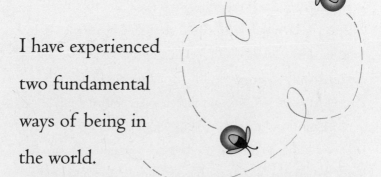

Until I became ill in my early thirties, I lived the normal life
of ego: looking out for No. 1, trying to preserve my habits
and defend my fixed worldview, and making bargains with
my fears in order to squeeze some enjoyment out of life.

The bridge from my old life to the new was

In this consciousness everything felt risky and there were few people I trusted. But I could always compare myself to someone less fortunate and feel like I was making out all right. After a seven-year health crisis that devastated my former sense of self, I found myself on a spiritual path. This meant I couldn't focus on looking out for No. I, because I wasn't sure of who or what I was anymore (or even if an "I" exists at all!). It meant entering a never-ending discipline of surrendering my habits and enlarging my worldview in the light of new information and insights.

Finally, it meant regarding fear as a common illusion—something to be honestly acknowledged, but never allowed to

forgiveness

dictate terms. In this consciousness, I increasingly feel cared for by an ineffable, pervasive intelligence that I sometimes call God, but often don't need to name at all. And I trust everyone to be doing the best they can to find that same kind of security, even if some are seriously misguided or tragically deluded in their pursuit of it. In a day-to-day sense, I don't know if my spiritual way of life is any easier than my old ego-driven way. Sometimes it's more demanding.

What has made the shift worthwhile is that my life makes sense to me now, and I feel consistently guided toward growth and service. In the old life I deeply doubted my worth and purpose, and secretly thought that I had too many unsolvable problems to be of real help to anyone. The bridge from my old life to the new was forgiveness: the complete release of my pained idea of who I was. This is the most important work I have ever done on my own behalf. In retrospect, I marvel at the victory I was earning during the time that I seemed to be suffering a total, grinding defeat.

Begin with the dull ache of a long-held shame. Don't try to argue away its justification; you've lost that argument many times already. Accept that your shame has helped

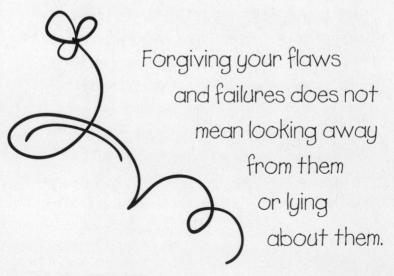

Forgiving your flaws
and failures does not
mean looking away
from them
or lying
about them.

make you who you are. Then compare your present sense of self to your sense of who you could be, who you've always wished to be, who you were born to be before you collided with the inevitable limitations and contradictions of this world. Between your shame and your ideal vision of yourself lies a great longing. Shift your attention to that longing—and then look back on your unforgiven shame. This is the first step out of pain and stagnation.

Forgiving your flaws and failures does not mean looking away from them or lying about them. Look at them as a string of pitiful or menacing hitchhikers whom you can't afford not to pick up on your journey to a changed life. Each of them has a piece of the map you need, hidden in its shabby clothing. You must listen attentively to all their stories and win the friendship of each one to put your map together. Where you are going—into a forgiven life of wholeness, passion, and commitment—you will need all the denizens of your dark side working diligently on your behalf.

I

A rage of frustration boiled over and you struck, changing your life and someone else's forever. There is an insult or injury you dealt that cannot be taken back or dismissed. This seems to be proof of your sinfulness, the personal stain that won't ever wash out. In fact it is the dye of your initiation into a more serious life. If you continue to live on automatic, you will do more damage. You must now learn to pay profound attention to your inner workings, which mirror the workings of the world at large. You must become an eminently practical, everyday philosopher of pain and redemption, changing your habits and exemplifying change for others as you go along. This is the work you chose for yourself when you attacked. It only begins with apologies and recompense.

II

When did you decide that you had the power to ruin your whole life? How do you know how much healing is possible? Are you in charge of all creation? Are you calling all the shots?

When I recognized the arrogance of believing I was doomed, I was chagrined in a way I had never felt before. This particular chagrin did not add to my burden of shame, but only helped dissolve it. To forgive myself I had to see clearly my errors of thinking and then truly release them, which meant giving up the expectation that I would continue to think stupidly. My habitual, circular thinking of shame and negativity stopped when I realized that it's not just me doing the thinking that counts. At my best I'm just translating creativity from a source beyond my comprehension. (Can anyone describe exactly how they get an idea, and where it comes from?) By keeping the channel of creativity as free as possible of shame, blame, and fear, I can achieve far more than I ever could by deliberate, rational efforts. Giving up the notions that I knew exactly who I was, and how great my failures were, actually enabled me to take charge of my life.

When there is nothing left
within us but love,
then forgiveness
has brought us to reality.

Self-hatred is nearly universal and takes many forms, from arrogance to false humility. Forgiveness teaches that we need not actually learn to "love ourselves" but instead to see that everything hateful or unloving within us is a tragic fiction that can be gently, firmly set aside. When there is nothing left within us but love, then forgiveness has brought us to reality.

Never forget that to forgive yourself is to release trapped energy that could be doing good work in the world. Thus, to judge and condemn yourself is a form of selfishness. Self-prosecution is never noble; it does no one a service.

Forgiveness induces a feeling of release, but it is actually a logical process—for you will not let go of the lamented past until you understand that continuing its suffering into the future is pointless.

Forgiveness feels most dramatic when some ancient pattern of self-punishment collapses in a torrent of tears. But it is just as effective when practiced daily in tiny doses—relinquishing a pointless worry, getting wise to a self-destructive habit, serving notice on a cruel notion about yourself that has previously seemed justified. The beginning of forgiveness is alertness to false ideas.

The essence of forgiveness is release, and only that which is false needs to be released. That's how I use forgiveness as an inner tool of self-development, constantly paring away the false from the true, the muddy from the

The essence
of forgiveness
is release,
and only that
which is false needs
to be released.

clear, the destructive from the useful. Applied to one's own consciousness, forgiveness is a sharp knife of discernment, and it may rapidly surpass the effects of countless hours of sit-down meditation or religious ritual. You have only to be willing to slice away the illusory roots of your personality, and briefly grieve the passing of the distorted images you have so long lived by. Then a new life, less limited by destructive habits and prejudices, can surface within you.

If your first attempts at self-forgiveness seem to change nothing in the way you feel, you are impatient for magic. Like an incantation, the steps of forgiving yourself may need many solemn repetitions before a door in your mind opens to real change. The change happens within you but comes from beyond you; you are only the Magician's helper.

I

Don't be fooled by the subtlety of some self-punishments, and do not mistake what is habitual for what is natural. Brooding, resenting, feeling bored, and frequently reviewing your laundry list of grumbles may seem like innocent reactions to a cruel world. In fact these are all ways in which your attention wanders away from healing.

II

Forgiveness brings order to your mind because it is the commitment to see everything—pain or pleasure, love or hatred, disaster or victory—in terms of the healing potential within. This decision is the key to a deep, abiding happiness that can sustain you through all passing sadnesses.

Forgiveness is a long night walk by the ocean at ebb tide, with the surf only murmuring.

I

Bad habits linger because they are unforgiven, not because one lacks willpower. Forgiving begins with appreciating the seriousness of the struggle that goes on while changing a habit. Your old familiar self will seldom yield gracefully to a new emerging one. To release a bad habit, never think of it as petty; changing a habit is actually the struggle to choose between a world of hurt and a world of healing. Paying exquisite attention will eventually enable you to let go of the deadening past, and rejoin the flow of your real life.

II

Every addiction is rooted in reluctance to shed some of the personality's coat of armor. The more willing we are to release our own defenses, the more spirit can come rushing in through the gaps in our armor.

III

To become completely free of addictions would be to lose all the barriers that separate us from each other. But don't worry about losing your personality; forgiveness will never rob you of what you truly need. As you discover that you prefer the feelings of freedom to those of self-defense, your capacity to handle freedom will increase.

To accelerate forgiveness, practice gratefulness. Every night, try to give equal thanks for all the day's events and encounters. When you discover yourself feeling grateful for things that seemed unpleasant when they occurred, you will be breaking the bonds of ordinary personality. You will soon no longer need to take pride in your wounds as a defense.

I was astonished when I began to appreciate my defeats, downturns, and disappointments. The sooner they were forgiven—that is, the sooner I gave up looking at them in the same old way—the more quickly my misfortunes seemed to add to my strength, alertness, and responsibility. As I began to perceive disappointment in a brighter light, I had to admit that "good" and "bad" events were getting harder and harder to tell apart. Lately it seems that bad things are merely those which I'm not yet prepared to handle effectively—and it also seems that they present themselves in order to help me increase my competence.

Forgiveness broadens your point of view and gives you see-through vision.

Forgiveness broadens your point of view and gives you see-through vision. Forgiveness floods your tiny resources of logic and rationality with an ocean of inspiration. You need only surrender the jealous guarding of your favorite, familiar frustrations.

Forgiveness replaces the need to anticipate fearfully with the capacity to accept gracefully and improvise brilliantly. It does not argue with fate, but recognizes the opportunities latent within it. If necessity is the mother of invention, forgiveness is the midwife of genius.

Learning is slowed less by lack of intelligence than by a reluctance to let go of bankrupt ideas and exhausted ways of seeing. This is why some problems never seem to go away even when their solutions are clearly within our grasp. When you feel cursed by fate, look to your own stubbornness; when you seem blocked by others' stupidity, question your own reasoning and the way you communicate. When nothing seems to work, consider whether you have correctly identified the fundamental problem behind your struggles. The object of your blame

You can get a lot more done in a typical day if you are not resisting life at every step of the way.

will always prove to be less of an obstacle than your decision to blame.

Forgiveness gradually enables you to deal directly and fully with all of your experiences and relationships, instead of cutting off those that seem to threaten pain or humiliation. In this sense, forgiveness is the key to versatility and openness.

You can get a lot more done in a typical day if you are not resisting life at every step of the way. A forgiving state of mind cannot easily be annoyed and does not waste time arguing with the unexpected.

If you are dreading an unwelcome challenge or event, you can forgive it in advance. This is not the same as merely hoping for the best, or praying for God to rescue you. Feeling dread means that you have begun planning for the future with fear as your chief advisor. Forgiveness fires that advisor and allows more helpful consultants—insight, ingenuity, chutzpah—to inform and inspire you.

I

Failure of the body provides a great temptation not to forgive, because forgiving may not soon halt the body's suffering. To understand this difficulty we must remember that the body itself is the first disability each of us experiences, and we have been angry with it ever since we were born hungry and wanting. Some religions reinforce this anger, warning that the body will demean our spirit unless it is punished and controlled. But not even the body can be convicted of wrongdoing on the basis of less than all the facts, and we live in a world rife with illusion and speculation. Learning to forgive the body may not cure our individual ills, but it will hasten the healing of the human condition. Anyone who learns to bear the body's suffering without anger is a noble missionary indeed.

II

Forgiveness effectively uses the body for communication and frees the body from being misused as an argument for loneliness.

III

Attacking the body is a distorted attempt to liberate the spirit, and glorifying the body is misplaced praise of spirit. Forgiveness corrects both errors without punishment.

I've always been fascinated by the fact that athletes who achieve the "zone" of peak performance often report that they hardly feel their bodies at all. For all the attention we pay to making the body feel better or look good, its health and attractiveness probably depend the most upon taking care of our spirit. Paradoxically, one way we learn to do that is by not misusing the body through neglect, punishment, or obsession. The key to spiritual growth is a kind and compassionate self-discipline, and sometimes that discipline has to be joyfully strenuous. The body presents us with our first training ground.

When you first decide to forgive yourself, you are stepping upon a great escalator headed up toward your potential. If you later decide to turn back, you will only stay where you are, until your renewed efforts at self-condemnation prove too exhausting to continue. If you decide to increase the escalator's pace with further efforts to understand and forgive yourself, you will see the gladdening sights up ahead just that much sooner.

The forgiven life is neither simple nor untroubled, and forgiveness does not prevent misfortunes. With practice, forgiveness does reduce the severity and frequency of the misfortunes that we tend to arrange for ourselves.

WHERE
FORGIVENESS
LEADS

Can we begin to
imagine a politics
of forgiveness?

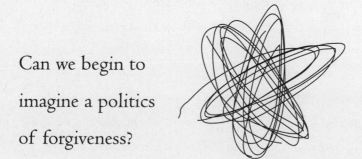

We've had the politics of one-upmanship, deception, and belligerence for so long that we may assume this way of doing things is human nature. If we believe that we must fight against our own nature to change our politics, then peace, justice, and human equality become romantic ideals that can never be achieved—although they can still be used as excuses for more war and sacrifice.

The extent to which we think world peace is possible is precisely the extent to which we think our own minds can someday be peaceful through and through. If we cannot comprehend why wars are fought over territories, national pride, or religious beliefs, then we need look no further than our fight for a parking space, the struggle to succeed against our competitors, or the aggressive ministry to convert one more soul to our church.

But human nature encompasses more than our destructive habits; it also has within it the potential for surrender. If we think of surrender as raising the white flag before our enemies, nothing within us will change. The surrender that matters is giving up the belief that we have any enemies. It doesn't matter whether humanity achieves that surrender tomorrow or a thousand years from now; simply remembering to make the attempt whenever possible is what will eventually undo the world as we know it.

How could our politics begin to express forgiveness? Imagine politicians debating publicly in order to learn from each other and educate the public, striving to outdo each other only on the attempt to make sure all parties have been fairly heard. Imagine the media hesitating in its rush to judgment of people and events—hesitating in order to place their reporting in the context of the most profound questions of human consciousness and moral evolution. Imagine our country's diplomatic envoys arguing for peace in international venues by admitting our warring history and tendencies first.

Are these radical departures from politics-as-usual really beyond human nature? Not if they are within our imagining—and if we can couple our imagination with an intense desire to end the human habit of alienation.

Forgiveness is one of the most undersold propositions of all time. When you first begin to grasp the potential of forgiveness, you will cheerfully trade all prior investments in aggression for the peace of its action.

Forgiveness blossoms at a certain moment in time, when you are ripe and ready to release some of the dead past. It is the intent to forgive that actually speeds up time, collapsing old schedules of suffering and bringing unimagined possibilities inestimably nearer.

Every act of forgiveness has the same nature but a unique expression. Your challenge is to create your particular style of forgiveness, then take it on the road.

Forgiveness unifies one's own awareness and will unite the consciousness of all humankind, which has been so long shattered into opposing egos, cultures, religions, and ideologies. Yet forgiveness also allows a creative diversity of ideas within one's own mind and instills a passionate tolerance of others' opinions and beliefs. Forgiveness will eventually preside over the raucous house of commons of the human soul, leading it with rigorous benevolence toward home.

Forgiveness blossoms
at a certain moment
in time,

when you are
ripe and ready
to release some
of the dead past.

I

Do not be misled by the myriad political faces of simple, stupid hatred. Whites and blacks hating each other, Arabs and Jews hating each other, Christians and Muslims, leftists and rightwingers—there was never any reason nor dignity to any of it. Every chronic hatred began when someone attacked, someone suffered, and no one forgave. Then these insane examples were multiplied and unwisely taught down through the generations. But the cycle of vengeance will never resolve itself. Someone has to step outside the cycle and courageously say, "I will take no pride in my tradition as long as it teaches martyrdom or revenge."

II

Beware also of hating the man who hates. Remember that you are here to help him lift off his yoke, not to boast that you stagger under one of a nobler design.

I've always been amazed by the power of bigots or hatemongers to arouse within me precisely the kind of hatred I despise within them. This is their real (if subconscious) agenda—not to further their race, culture, or beliefs, but to clone their inward misery in the consciousness of others, and thus feel less alone. Ultimately this is a self-defeating strategy, but it gains a little credence every time the hater can inspire any kind of hatred within another person, regardless of whether it's a hatred that supports or opposes his cause. To understand the hater, I need look no further than my revulsion in his presence. And I have to look at this revulsion steadily, continuously, courageously—until I see exactly how my own loneliness has crafted such a fearsome mask. Then I am a step closer to understanding how bigotry might be undone.

Forgiveness does not mean letting error and evil continue unchecked, but it does require us to help each other trace all our errors to their source: the fear that we have been abandoned here to die. In countless forms, this anxiety creates all the despair of the world. By striving to surrender the belief in abandonment, anyone can practice resurrection.

Anger exiles hope to the mind's dark and stuffy attic, cluttered with nostalgic curiosities. Forgiveness clears a space in the mind where hope finds enough room to devise practical strategies of change.

Forgiveness sends a healing message much further than you might believe. As you develop a forgiving demeanor, you become an automatic transmitter within the network of human consciousness—changing minds less by your words than by your example, saving souls less by your program than by your presence.

A conviction is a strong and fixed belief; to be convicted is to be found guilty of something. There is more than a semantic connection between belief and guilt. Whenever we believe we know something for sure in this uncertain, paradoxical world, we will be perilously close to convicting ourselves or others of unpardonable crimes. Forgiveness gradually and carefully relieves us of our dependence on *believing*, increasingly enabling us just to *be*. Then our actions can arise from an instinctive wisdom that draws from our practical knowledge, yet transcends our limited grasp of truth.

Forgiveness is a curious paradox of accepting everything just as it is while working tirelessly for a complete upheaval in our behavior and consciousness. Some activists believe we must be constantly aggrieved to set right the injustices of the world—that good anger corrects bad anger. But an enlightened activism respectfully acknowledges all anger and sorrow while demonstrating the superior strategy of mercy, pooling ever deeper within and rhythmically flowing without. The most effective and lasting actions arise from profound stillness and radical clarity.

Ultimately, forgiveness means letting go of this world, a darkened, fractured glass through which we see love only dimly. As our frightened grip on all that is temporary relaxes, we will increasingly find our authentic strength in that which is timeless, boundless, inexhaustible, and omnipresent. Heaven is learned, not simply entered with religion's passport.

Forgiveness is not mere sympathy, nor condescension, nor forced generosity. It is the ultimate declaration of equality, founded on the recognition that all crimes are the same crime, every failing the human failing, and every insult a cry for help.

The only way to remain angry at someone is to refuse to look into what may have caused that person to perpetuate a crime or injury. If you thoroughly investigate anyone's motivations, you will eventually find the sense, however twisted, behind all destructive acts. It will boil down to one of two purposes: Either people think that causing others suffering will ease their own, or they believe that everyone deserves only suffering. These mistaken beliefs drive the world as we know it, and I doubt that anyone is entirely free of them. When I recognize these errors in myself or someone who tempts my anger, I try to remember that I want to learn and teach something new. I can hardly judge or punish others for their mixed-up motivations before I have straightened out my own.

Forgiveness is a strong, steady rain washing away drought.

I

A shock is felt when you realize that you have mistaken cynicism for sophistication, and that very little of what you have so long and bitterly believed is true. For you have hoarded only the evidence that fit your theories of attack and preserved your misery. In your changing vision, all that evidence is evaporating like a mist. This can be highly embarrassing—what if your friends see you losing all your vaunted toughness? But forgiveness doesn't particularly care about your reputation.

II

Or you think you are always gentle, yet look at how viciously the world strikes at you nonetheless! This idea of your victimization is merely cynicism turned inside out and made more impenetrable to insight. You are clever enough to disguise your addiction to gloom in protests of innocence. The good news is that you may never be effectively challenged by others about this routine; few friends have enough wisdom and willingness to confront you at the same time. The bad news is that you will probably never walk your way to forgiveness in sensible steps. You will have to leap your own well-built defenses, disowning your morbid vanity in mid-flight.

Forgiveness is a science of the heart: a discipline of discovering all the ways of being that will extend your love to the world, and discarding all the ways that do not.

I

As forgiveness liberates your energy, you may be moved to sing, dance, write, make art, or otherwise celebrate. Don't let your day job get in the way.

II

As forgiveness liberates your thinking, you may find yourself looking beyond the world-wearying drives of self-promotion and competition. Congratulations! Now you are consciously evolving, no longer running the treadmill of humanity's favorite follies. Now you will be led by inspiration everywhere you are needed.

THE
SEVEN STEPS
EXPANDED

Over the years
since this book
was first published,
I've become aware that readers could use more specific
suggestions about implementing the Seven Steps of
Forgiving. So I am repeating them here with some practical tips on making the most of each step. You can use
this section as a study guide for yourself or a group
focused on forgiveness work.

It's about recognizing that everything in your experience that seems less than good can be seen differently, and ultimately transformed.

Every one of these steps can be enhanced or accelerated with the use of a journal. At times of crisis in my own
life, I have written book-length journals strictly for my own
use in transcending the challenges I was facing. A forgiveness journal doesn't have to be full of nice sentiments. In
fact, for long stretches it may be just the opposite, as you
allow the full expression of every feeling or idea that is
standing in the way of your growth or happiness.
Forgiveness is not about being or sounding good.

But first you have to recognize everything, good and
bad, that makes up the whole of what you are. Other
forms of expression—music, painting, dance, toothpick
sculptures—may also help you illuminate your own process
of forgiveness. I've learned that creativity always follows in
the wake of forgiveness, even if you don't see the connection at first. Great challenges may stop you in your tracks
for a while. But if you meet them with forgiveness, you will
eventually find yourself propelled forward again with an
inspiration that may properly be called divine.

1

Select a bitter sorrow, a serious grievance against someone, or a punishing charge against yourself, and review it in complete detail.

If you are holding a grudge or nursing a long-held sorrow, you may have actually forgotten some of the details of the event or circumstances that created the problem. Behind the chronic attachment to any particular pain is often an incomplete story. For instance, you may not be looking at the problem from all sides—especially the side of anyone who seems to have perpetrated something against you. To look at things from the side of your "enemy" is not to sympathize against yourself, but to understand more clearly how someone came to do what they did. When you begin to grasp someone else's logic (however flawed it may be), your wisdom is increased, and you will be gifted with new insights and solutions for change.

One way to review what you intend to forgive is to write it down as a story in the third person, seeing yourself as just one of the players in a network of relationships and events rather than the central victim (or perpetrator). Imagine that you have a treetop perspective "above the battleground" of what happened, and see if your idea of what happened changes as you record the story from this new vantage point. If you're inclined to another form of expression than writing, use the same perspective to compose a song, draw a picture, or do whatever appeals to you. You can also simply re-imagine the history of your grievance in your mind without recording it. Trying this more than once may yield some interesting variations.

Whatever you do, watch your dreams over the weeks and months to come. When you consciously activate the process of forgiveness, your unconscious will go to work as well, and some startling new insights may soon surface.

2

Hold in your mind the image of
whatever is to be forgiven—yourself,
ther person, a past event—and
release you from the grip of my
s, disapproval, or
nation." Concentrate quietly
tion.

In most cases, what prolongs our psychic pain is not what actually happened to us in the past, but the particular way in which we are holding on to it—that is, the "grip" on the past that we have come to maintain without realizing it. To release that grip is not to forget what happened, or to make excuses for yourself or another person. Instead, it means relaxing your mental and emotional fixation on the pain, in order to let another kind of energetic response arise within you. When you first attempt this step, you may experience resistance within yourself. In fact, it would be surprising if you didn't. However much resistance arises, don't struggle with it; just note it and let it be, then try the step again later. This step succeeds every time you attempt it, because it is only about establishing your intention to forgive. Repeating and renewing that intention gives it increasing power. You don't have to make it work; the intention to forgive eventually transforms your awareness on its own.

3

Imagine for a while what your life will be like without the sorrow or grievance that has been haunting you.

Part of any chronic disturbance about the past is the resentful belief that our future has been damaged or limited. While your physical or material circumstances can certainly be changed or permanently affected by something that happened to you, the quality of your consciousness at any given moment is always up to you. If you are haunted by the past, then the part of your mind that holds your future will be dim and ghostly. If you can imagine being

If you can imagine being free of anger and grief, then the future can lighten up.

free of anger and grief, then the future can lighten up. Do not confuse this step with wishful thinking or wistful fantasizing. It requires taking a break from negative habits of thinking, and assessing your potential as a person liberated by forgiveness. A practical way to do this is to make a list of what you could do if you were free:

If I were not sad or angry about

_____

_____,

then I would be able to . . .

_____

_____

_____

_____

and then write down whatever comes to mind, in terms of your untapped potentials or blocked capacities. Keep the list handy so that you can add to it whenever a new possibility occurs to you. You may be surprised at some of the ideas that crop up, and all the untapped powers that are waiting in the wings of your awareness. Who knows—the list of your potentials may become so inviting that you can't resist bringing them to life!

4

Make amends with someone you've hurt or someone who has hurt you; tell a friend about your self-forgiveness; or otherwise bring your inner work to your relationships.

The first stage of forgiveness may be entirely interior, as you refocus your mind on a new way of thinking and perceiving. This stage should not be rushed. But eventually you will reach a point where you need to carry your inner work into your relationships. This can be as simple as telling someone that you'd like to bring peace to an argument you've been having, or apologizing for something you've said or done. You can say this in person, make a call, or write a letter. Whatever your approach may be, this step must be firmly grounded in the realization that everyone gains from the process of forgiveness.

Yet you should not be impatient for a miraculous shift in the quality of an aggrieved relationship. Another person may not be as ready to forgive and move on as you are—or you may discover that there is something missing or unfinished in your own approach. Forgiveness is a constant reeducation, and that process is often accelerated in the presence of anyone with whom you have issues of anger,

This can be as simple as telling someone that you'd like to bring peace to an argument you've been having, or apologizing for something you've said or done.

sadness, or disappointment. Even when you are working solely on forgiving yourself, it can be very helpful to have someone in whom you can confide your realizations and changing point of view. Over time, you may feel inspired to share what you are learning with a group, a social network, or an audience. You might even end up writing a book.

5

Ask for God's help to overcome fear or resistance at any step. If you do not believe in God, ask for help from nature, humanity, and the mysteries of your own mind. These are the channels through which aid is sent— and aid is always sent.

Forgiveness is a spiritual process,

but by no means does it have to be pursued in a religious context. When you have a comfortable relationship with a divine intelligence that you may call God, then the idea of asking for help from beyond yourself will already be familiar. If not, then you may find this kind of resource in nature. In this book you will find three references to experiences in nature that helped me transcend the difficulties of forgiveness when it felt like slow going. You may also turn to trusted friends and advisors, art or literature, a meditation practice, or the suggestions of your own dreams. When you begin to look for help in forgiving, you will tend to discover allies and resources of which you were previously unaware.

The reason that "aid is always sent" is because forgiveness is a request that answers itself. I've come to believe that forgiveness is actually an instinct, long-buried in many people but nonetheless ready to come to the fore when summoned. Forgiveness is not quite the same as love, but it does open the door to love. When that door has been opened and you are ready to step over the threshold, you will recognize that you have finally returned home.

Forgiveness is not
quite the same as
love, but it does
open the door to

6

Have patience. Forgiveness induces healing which follows its own order and timing. Whether you think you have accomplished anything thus far is less important than the fact that you have attempted a radical act that will call forth change likely to exceed your expectations. Go about your daily business, but stay alert to unexpected shifts in your thinking, feelings, and relationships.

Forgiveness is a mystical process.

That means it works on many levels of our psyches and relationships at once, some of which we will not be aware. I've noticed that when I've been working for a while with a "big" forgiveness issue on which I don't seem to be making much progress, then some of the less significant problems of my life get easier or disappear entirely. It's as if forgiveness is a kind of aspirin that's not strong enough to stop a migraine, but takes care of some other nagging aches and pains nonetheless.

But I think what's really happening is that the process of learning to forgive is enabling me to release some of the smaller annoyances of life while I keep holding on to bigger problems—until I understand that I really don't need any of those problems to know who I am. Thus, it's important to remember that inviting forgiveness into your mind always

has effects, even if you are not aware of them for a while. It's not so much a matter of having faith in forgiveness, as being open to change and surprise.

Just as you can sometimes see a dim cluster of stars more clearly by looking off to the side than directly at it, you may first become aware of forgiveness working on the edges of your self-awareness. Sooner or later, forgiveness will seep through to your center.

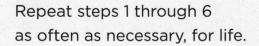

7

Repeat steps 1 through 6
as often as necessary, for life.

Forgiveness is an ongoing process,

not a singular achievement. As you gain experience, you may apply the steps I've provided in a different order and with different kinds of emphasis, and you will no doubt invent more steps or even shortcuts of your own. Although forgiveness can feel awkward and unnatural when first undertaken, over time it becomes a new way of relating to people and to the unpredictable course of one's life. Then it becomes less necessary to practice forgiveness as a discipline, because it has become a natural response to every difficulty.

I'm sometimes surprised nowadays when I see people reacting with anger to minor annoyances or unexpected events, and I realize that years ago I would have reacted similarly—but not now. That's not because I've become a saint (or resigned to fate), but because I can more easily integrate the twists and turns of life and relationships than I used to. Paradoxically, the more you develop a forgiving demeanor, the less there is to forgive.

ACKNOWLEDGMENTS

This book has a long history, and to thank everyone who played a part in its evolution would be an impossible task. I will mention everyone I can think of, and hope that the rest may find a way to forgive me (see page 1). Helpful readers of the original manuscript included my parents, the late Lester and Janie Miller; Tom Rusk MD; Ann LyonBoutelle; J. Ruth Gendler; Billie Fitzpatrick; and especially Laurie Fox. Linda Chester, founder of the agency Laurie works with, took this work to heart and skillfully navigated the shoals and whirlpools of Manhattan's publishing world to help the book find its first home at Viking. There, editor Caroline White accurately saw how the original draft could be improved, and her insights and guidance still grace the current edition. In recent years, I have been supported and further educated in the process of forgiveness by many remarkable people, including the late Kenneth Wapnick, Gary Renard and his mystic advisors, all the fine folks in my erstwhile ACIM study group, Thuy-Nhien Vuong, Sharon Sherrard, and Sari Friedman. And a final thanks to Hampton Roads publisher Greg Brandenburgh for recognizing that this book had one more life to live.

ABOUT THE AUTHOR

D. PATRICK MILLER is an author, editor, and
literary agent specializing in contemporary spirituality.
A native of Charlotte, North Carolina, Miller now lives
in northern California. You can contact him at
www.fearlessbooks.com.

Hampton Roads Publishing Company

. . . for the evolving human spirit

Hampton Roads Publishing Company
publishes books on a variety of subjects,
including spirituality, health, and other related topics.

For a copy of our latest trade catalog,
call (978) 465-0504 or visit our
distributor's website at *www.redwheelweiser.com.*
You can also sign up for our newsletter
and special offers by going to
www.redwheelweiser.com / newsletter /.